Nowhere to Hide: Selections on Cybersecurity and Politics

Restoring the African Mind Research
Collection

1 NOWHERE TO HIDE: THE DANGERS OF GOVERNMENT SURVEILLANCE

Digital technology has helped to connect us and provide easy access to information. In doing so, digital technology has also made government surveillance on our lives much easier. This issue has become a very contentious one in the United States since it was uncovered that the National Security Agency (NSA) has been spying on American citizens and compiling that information. There are laws to protect American citizens against warrantless searches, but these laws are only effective after the fact. Neil M. Richards explained: "Although we have laws that protect us against government surveillance, secret government programs cannot be challenged until they are discovered. And even when they are, our law of surveillance provides only minimal protections. Courts frequently dismiss challenges to such programs for lack of standing, under the theory that mere surveillance creates no harms."

An example of this was *Al-Haramain Islamic Foundation, Inc. v. Bush* in which the government successfully invoked the state-secrets doctrine to prevail. The ruling of this case held that if plaintiffs could not prove that their calls had been listened to then they could not establish standing to sue for violations of their civil liberties. In other words, plaintiffs have to be able to prove that the government has been monitoring them, but this is not something that the American government would admit to.

Another legal challenge which faces the targets of government surveillance is proving harm. This was the issue in *ACLU v. NSA*, in which the Sixth Circuit dismissed the claim that First Amendment values were threatened by the government listening to private conversations. The court ruled that the plaintiffs had no standing to assert either a First or Fourth Amendment violation since the plaintiffs were unable to prove that the government's surveillance program had targeted them.

The American government would obviously argue that the purpose of surveillance is to protect the public, but given the nation's history, there certainly is cause for concern. The United States is a nation with its own history of political persecution against political activists. The F.B.I. in particular has a history of targeting black activists who challenged racism in the United States. This resulted in many of these activists either being assassinated or imprisoned. Even with this history, there seems to be a feeling among some that government surveillance in the United States does not pose an immediate threat to the public at large. The previously mentioned court rulings would indicate this point. Richards explained that "few critics of government surveillance such as the NSA wiretapping program and the British data-retention regulations would suggest that these programs are directly analogous to the evil regime depicted in Orwell's dystopia. Moreover, the Orwell metaphor seems wholly inapplicable to databases used to personalize targeted advertising on the web, the efforts of insurance companies to promote safe driving, and the practices of online booksellers to sell more books by monitoring consumers' shopping habits in ways that used to be impossible."

Richards is critical of the failure by American courts "to recognize that a reasonable fear of government surveillance threatens the privacy of the surveilled, causing them to act differently." American courts seem to hold the view that government surveillance is not a serious threat to the American public because such spying typically does not result in an adverse action. The situation would perhaps be different if warrantless surveillance by the American government led to acts of repression against political opponents. This is precisely the issue in Togo, where the government has used surveillance to maintain its oppressive rule.

Citizen Lab reported in 2020 that the government of Togo had used NSO spyware to target Togolese civil society, including religious leaders and opposition politicians. NSO Group is an Israeli spyware developer. In 2019, WhatsApp identified and fixed a vulnerability which allowed attackers to inject NSO Group spyware onto phones. At least 1,400 WhatsApp users were targeted in this incident. Citizen Lab conducted an investigation after this attack which uncovered that citizens in Togo were among those who were targeted in the attack in 2019. This included a bishop, a priest, and two members of the political opposition in

Togo. Among the opposition leaders who were targeted was Elliott Ohin, who previously served in the government.

In Togo, there is a history of government repression of those who speak out against the regime. One of the most notable examples of this is the assassination of Tavio Amorin, who was a prominent critic of the dictatorship in Togo. The internet became a powerful tool for activists because it allowed them to speak out against the dictatorship in Togo while also maintaining their anonymity. Farida Nabourema noted: "I was one of those activists, and like many of my fellow dissidents I have felt empowered in the years since Mr. Gnassingbé's rise by the ability to denounce the government — its corruption and gangsterism — on social media. 'You may rule over Togo with no accountability,' I wrote in a 2014 Facebook post, addressing the administration, 'but we citizens rule over the internet, and we will hold you accountable.'"

As it would turn out, Gnassingbé's government would not tolerate this digital resistance to his regime. The first indication of this was the government's response to the protests in 2017. The government decided to shut down the internet for nine days. In the months that followed, hundreds of protesters were arrested and some were killed.

Cutting off the internet or restricting internet access has become a common tactic used by repressive African governments to stifle their population. This was done by Joseph Kabila in the Democratic Republic of Congo to stifle protests there. In Tanzania, President John Magufuli introduced regulations that would charge bloggers over $900 to publish their content, which was done as part of Magufuli's effort to stifle criticism of his government.

In January 2019, Zimbabwe underwent a severe bout of civil unrest, triggered by a government decree to raise fuel prices. The protests that followed rapidly spread nationwide, reflecting deeper frustrations with economic collapse, high inflation, scarce foreign currency, deteriorating public services, and perceptions of political mismanagement. As part of its response, the Zimbabwean government imposed a total internet shutdown, cutting off access to the internet, including widely used social media platforms like Facebook, Twitter, and WhatsApp. This clampdown on digital communications occurred amid reports of violent state repression as authorities sought to quell the unrest.

It would eventually become apparent that the Togolese government was able to ascertain the identities of certain activists through digital spying. Nabourema stated, "we received information suggesting that some activists had been arrested and tortured by the government based on evidence gleaned from private conversations that had taken place on WhatsApp, the encrypted messaging app. This gave us a strong hint that the government was spying on us, thus destroying our anonymity as online activists and putting our own security and that of our family members in jeopardy. I was in contact with some of the imprisoned activists for months; many were subsequently forced to flee the country or to go into hiding."

The situation in Togo demonstrates the threat posed by government surveillance under a dictatorial regime. The government of the United States eventually came to recognize the threat posed by the NSO Group which the Togolese government relied on for its spyware. This was why the American government blacklisted NSO Group in 2021. This was a significant step towards curbing the abuses being carried out internationally by spyware, but more still needs to be done to combat the abuses being committed by governments such as the one in Togo.

Selected References:

David E. Sanger, Nicole Perlroth, Ana Swanson and Ronen Bergman, "U.S. Blacklists Israeli Firm NSO Group Over Spyware," *New York Times*, 2021.

Farida Nabourema, "In Togo, There is Nowhere to Hide," *New York Times*, 2020.

John Scott-Railton, Siena Anstis, Sharly Chan, Bill Marczak, and Ron Deibert, "Nothing Sacred: Religious and Secular Voices for Reform in Togo Targeted with NSO Spyware," *The Citizen Lab*, 2020.

Neil M. Richards, "The Dangers of Surveillance," *Harvard Law*

Review, 2013.

2 UNDERSTANDING THE DANGERS OF SOCIAL ENGINEERING ATTACKS

One of the most effective ways to compromise a security system is by compromising the individuals who operate the system. This is precisely what social engineering attacks do. Social engineering refers to psychologically manipulating a target into doing what the attacker wants the target to do. A common type of social engineering is known as phishing. There are several types of phishing attacks which are listed below:

- Phishing: Phishing involves an attempt to obtain sensitive information from the user by pretending to be a trusted entity. An example of this is an attacker pretending to be a representative of a bank in order to obtain the banking information of the target. These attacks are often delivered by email. This is a form of social engineering combined with spoofing. The goal of a phishing attack is to trick the victim into providing sensitive information.
- Vishing: Vishing is a type of phishing attack which is done via a phone rather than through email. The method and goal of a vishing attack is much like that of a phishing attack in that the attackers impersonate someone else in order to obtain important information from the victim.
- Smishing: Smishing or SMS phishing is a phishing attack which is carried out via mobile text messaging.
- Spear phishing: Spear phishing is a type of phishing attack which targets a particular individual. Spear phishing may involve any of the three abovementioned methods. The goal of spear phishing is to target a specific person, as opposed to an attack which is aimed at multiple targets. Whaling is a type of spear phishing attack which targets a high-profile individual such as a CEO.

In addition to phishing schemes, another common execution of social engineering is a watering hole attack. This attack targets a popular website where users are known to visit. This attack gets its name from a watering hole, which is a body of water where animals go to drink. Pretexting is another type of social engineering attack. Pretexting involves a situation, or pretext, created by an attacker in order to lure a victim into a vulnerable situation and to trick them into giving private information.

Social engineering attacks rely on certain important principles. One of which is the power of authority. People tend to obey authority figures. Stanley Milgram's experiment demonstrated that individuals will obey authority figures even when they are requested to do things that they are uncomfortable with doing. In the experiment, Milgram had participants read a list of questions to a respondent. If the respondent answered incorrectly, the participant was requested to give an electric shock to the respondent. The participant was made to increase the voltage with each wrong answer. The participants did not know that the respondent was an actor who was pretending to be shocked. As far as the participants knew, they were really electrocuting the respondent. Participants who were clearly distressed at inflicting pain, still continued with the experiment. Two-thirds of the volunteers were prepared to administer a potentially fatal electric shock.

Milgram was inspired to conduct this experiment by the Nuremberg trials of Nazi officials who claimed they were "just following orders." Milgram wanted to explore the psychological mechanisms of obedience. What he discovered was shocking, but his experiment demonstrated the power of authority.

There are other principles as well, such as liking. People are easily persuaded by individuals that they like. Whereas authority relies on the manipulator presenting himself or herself as an authority figure, liking is designed to put the target at ease by making the target believe that the manipulator is a likable individual.

Social proof is another one. This is based on the notion that people will do things that they see other people doing. If everyone else is doing it, then it must be something worth doing. This method relies on getting the target to believe that a particular action is socially acceptable.

Scareware is a tactic which is used to trick the target into believing that he or she has been infected with malware. The purpose of doing this is to scare the target into thinking that he or she needs to buy or install software to resolve the problem. The goal is to get the target to install fake software which will actually infect the device. These scareware attacks usually appear as pop-up security alerts. These alerts appear to be legitimate warnings that the computer has been infected, but they are really fake alerts which are designed to scare the target.

Social engineering attacks can be very effective and very costly, as demonstrated by the attack carried out by Evaldas Rimasauskas. Rimasauskas, who is a Lithuanian national, carried out an attack in which he targeted Google and Facebook from 2013 to 2015. Rimasauskas' scheme involved a fake business entity. He registered and operated a company in Latvia that bore the same name as Quanta Computer, a legitimate Taiwan-based hardware supplier that worked with major tech firms. He sent carefully crafted phishing emails to employees at Google and Facebook who were responsible for processing vendor invoices.

These emails which Rimasauskas sent contained realistic-looking invoices, contracts, and other corporate documentation that appeared to come from the legitimate Quanta Computer. Given that both companies actually had a business relationship with the real Quanta, the fraudulent communications raised no immediate suspicion. As a result, employees wired large sums of money into bank accounts controlled by Rimasauskas in Latvia and Cyprus. Over $100 million was transferred over to Rimasauskas before the scheme was overcovered.

There are important steps that can be taken to avoid being the victim of a social engineering attack. One of which is not opening emails and attachments which are sent from unknown sources. Do not provide sensitive information to unknown sources either.

Tempting offers should also be viewed with caution. These attacks can be especially effective since manipulators can get what they want from their targets by telling their targets what they want to hear. For example, a common phishing attack method involves promises of money. I have even read about scams involving people claiming to be publishing companies who arc willing to publish the books of aspiring authors.

Ensuring that you have installed antivirus and that all of the software on your device is updated is important for ensuring the security of your devices, but social engineering is designed to bypass these security measures through manipulating the target. This is why being informed and alert when encountering social engineering attempts is important.

3 THINK LIKE A HACKER: MOTIVES AND METHODS

Being able to think like a hacker can be a very effective method to protect yourself from cyberattacks. In this short essay, I will explore some of the different things that motivate hackers and some of the techniques which hackers use to achieve their aims to give the reader some insight into what hackers do and what motivates hackers to do what they do.

It is important to note that there are different types of hackers and not all hackers are bad actors. There are what are known as white hat hackers. These are hackers who use their abilities to help protect others from hackers. A common occupation for a white hat hacker would be what is known as penetration testing. This is when a hacker hacks into a device or a system with the permission of the owner. This is done for the purpose of finding weaknesses and vulnerabilities which need to be patched so as to avoid being exploited by a malicious hacker.

Black hat hackers are hackers who hack with malicious intent. This includes criminals who utilize ransomware for money or hackers who steal passwords to gain access to an individual's bank account. Finally, there are gray hat hackers. Gray hat hackers are individuals who engage in illegal hacking, but for noble purposes. An example of this would be a hacker who looks for vulnerabilities in a system without an owner's permission, but rather than exploiting these vulnerabilities, the hacker reports them to the owner. Hackers who hack for political reasons may be also regarded as gray hat hackers. Such hackers are also known as hacktivists. The cause for which hacktivists utilize their hacking skills for may be a noble cause, but hacking into the device of an individual without the consent of said individual is still illegal nevertheless.

The entity that is responsible for carrying out the cyberattack is known as a threat actor. There are different types of threat actors with different motivations for why they engage in cyberattacks. One of the most dangerous types of threat actors are insider threats, such as employees or contractors who work for an organization. These threats are especially dangerous because they are already inside of the network.

Criminal syndicates are groups which engage in hacking for illegal purposes. This is typically done with the goal of obtaining money. By far the most powerful threat actor is the nation state actor. This typically refers to governments who employ hacking for their own political agendas. Nation state actors have the largest amount of resources at their disposal. These resources are used to spy on other governments and in many instances to spy on citizens as well. Dictatorial regimes, especially, tend to utilize their technological capacity to spy on and suppress activists. Nation state actors may also employ criminal syndicates to carry out hacking on behalf of the nation state. These would be referred to as state sponsored hackers.

By far the least threatening type of threat actor on the list is a script kiddie. This is not to imply that script kiddies are not a serious threat, however. The term script kiddie—which is somewhat demeaning—refers to someone who is simply running a script to perform a hack. A script kiddie is not capable of creating their own script and often does not even know how the scripts that they are using work. Script kiddies are typically motivated to hack out of curiosity, for entertainment, or even for money. Script kiddies are typically inexperienced and have limited resources, but, as I stated, this does not mean that script kiddies are not a serious threat. A script kiddie who is able to get access to ransomware, for example, can pose a serious threat to companies.

Now that we have briefly looked at some of the types of hackers who are out there, we will next look at the different methods which hackers use and some of the ways to protect yourself from these methods. There are different types of cyberattacks which hackers engage in to achieve their motives. I will start with password-based attacks since passwords are the most common way that the average user on the internet secures their digital information. Things like bank accounts, medical information, and other private documents can often be obtained simply through gaining access to an individual's password.

One of the ways that an attacker can get access to your account is my simply forcing their way in through guessing your password.

This is known as a brute force attack. In a brute force attack an attacker submits many passwords or passphrases with the hope of eventually guessing correctly. The attacker systematically checks all possible passwords and passphrases until the correct one is found.

Another password attack is a dictionary attack. This type of attack is so named because it relies on using a list of words that one would find in a dictionary. This method is especially effective for cracking passwords which are a single word. For example, the password "password" can very easily be cracked by a dictionary attack.

Some attackers will try a spraying attack. This is done to avoid the problem of being locked out for too many login attempts. The attacker will use one password against many different accounts on the application to avoid account lockouts that would normally occur when brute forcing a single account with many passwords. In other words, instead of spending time and effort to target one account, the hacker will target several accounts with the same password to see if one of the passwords works.

One of the most basic ways that you can protect yourself is by avoiding the use of weak passwords. An example of a weak password would be "12345." This is very easily guessed. Other examples would be passwords involving your own name, such as "Dwayne123." Typically, a strong password will include a mix of letters—both upper and lower case—in addition to numbers and symbols. Passwords should also avoid utilizing personal information such as your name or your date of birth because these things can be easily guessed if the hacker has personal knowledge about you

Software refers to a set of instructions which tell a computer how to operate. Malware is a type of software which is designed for the purpose of causing damage to a computer. Malware is typically utilized by hackers to carry out their cyberattacks.

Viruses are among the most commonly used types of malware. A virus is a malicious code which replicates itself by attaching itself to another piece of executable code. Once the code is executed, the virus is executed as well. Worms are pieces of code which attempt to penetrate networks and computer systems. Unlike viruses, worms can survive without attaching themselves to another piece of code, such as a file. This means that the user does not need to execute anything to activate a worm. Once a worm manages to penetrate into a system, it can replicate itself and spread to other computers.

A trojan horse is a type of malware which is very difficult to detect because it disguises itself as code which is not malicious. Trojan malware takes its name from the Trojan Horse which was used in the Trojan War. According to the story, the Greeks abandoned their position and left behind a large wooden horse. The Trojans believed that the Greeks had surrendered and they decided to take the horse into their city as a trophy. What the Trojan warriors did not know is that inside the large wooden horse were Greek warriors. That night, the Greeks who were hiding inside of the horse snuck out and opened the gates of the city of Troy, which allowed the Greek army to ambush and destroy the city. Trojan malware operates under the same principle of disguising itself as something not threatening. This is done to avoid detection from malware scanners and firewalls.

Ransomware is another common type of malware which is increasingly becoming a serious problem for American companies. Ransomware is a type of malware which, as the name implies, takes data for ransom. Ransomware does this by encrypting files on a system thereby leaving the files unusable until the ransom is paid. This type of malware would typically be used by criminal syndicates to obtain money.

Ransomware attacks are often carried out through sending malicious emails to the target. This is why it is a good practice not to open any links or attachments in emails which come from unknown sources. Of course, some hackers can be very effective at tricking the target into thinking that the email is coming from a legitimate source. It is always a good idea to have a backup for important data as well, so that you are able to maintain access to the data in the event that you are targeted by a ransomware attack.

In addition to ransomware, there are also ransom denial of service attacks. Whereas ransomware crypto-locks data, ransom denial of service disrupts a business' online services. In cybersecurity a denial of service (DOS) attack refers to an attack which is intended to disrupt a users' ability to connect to a network. This is typically accomplished by flooding the targeted machine with information to overload the system. There is also a distributed denial of service (DDOS) attack, which is more sophisticated because it involves using multiple different systems to overwhelm the target.

A ransom DOS attack is one in which the hacker targets a business until the business pays the ransom. An example of this might be a DOS attack aimed at shutting down the website of a business which relies on the internet for the majority of its business. Doing so essentially holds the business hostage because the business would not be able to engage in its normal functions until the DOS ends.

Botnets are a group of internet-connected devices which run bots. These bots can be used to carry out various types of attacks, such as a distributed denial of service (DDOS) attack or data stealing. Botnets can be controlled by the owner using command and control (C&C) software. In some cases, your device can become infected and become part of the botnet, which means that the attacker has taken control of your device and is now using the device to conduct the attack.

Spyware is a type of malware which is used to spy on the activities of the target. Spyware can be used to monitor and record what is being done on the infected devices. One type of spyware is known as a keylogger. Keyloggers, as the name suggests, captures and logs the keystrokes on your computer. This can be used for ascertaining passwords. As noted before, there are a number of methods to illegally obtain a person's password, but a keylogger makes this process very easy since passwords may be entered in an encrypted form, but the keystrokes are not encrypted. One of the ways to counter the use of a keylogger is to enter all of your passwords via the digital on-screen keyboard on your computer. This can prevent some forms of keyloggers from capturing the keystrokes from your keyboard, but this is not a guarantee against all types of keyloggers, as some keyloggers can capture information from the digital keyboard.

Backdoors are originally designed as methods used by software developers to ensure that they could gain access to an application even if something were to happen that would prevent normal access methods. One example of this is a hard-coded password that could be used to gain access to the program in the event that administrations forgot their own system password. The problem here is that if it is hard-coded then it cannot be removed. If a hacker were to get ahold of this password, then there would be no way to prevent a hacker from gaining access to this application. Backdoors are created as ways to allow the software developers to gain access, but it can also be used by hackers. Once they are inside, hackers can use a backdoor to steal personal and financial data, install additional malware, and hijack devices. Backdoor also refers to programs that attackers install after gaining unauthorized access to a system to ensure that they can continue to have unrestricted access to the system, even if their initial access method is discovered and blocked.

Logic bombs are a type of malicious software which is deliberately installed by an authorized user, such as an employee. A logic bomb is designed to remain dormant for a period of time until it is triggered, either by a particular event or it can be designed to be set off on a particular date. A common example of a logic bomb would be a disgruntled employee who implements a logic bomb to activate after he has been fired from the company. Logic bombs can be difficult to detect because they are often installed by authorized users.

In addition to malware which is used to carry out cyberattacks, hackers also utilize what is known as wireless attacks. These are attacks which utilize wireless connections to compromise a person's system. An example of this would be what is known as an evil twin attack. This attack gets its name because it involves the attacker setting up a fraudulent wireless access point which mimics the characteristics of a legitimate access point. An example of this would be a hacker who sets up a Wi-Fi connection in a crowded location such as an airport. The hacker may set up a hotspot using the same SSID name as the real network to trick guests into signing into the fake SSID. From here the hacker can then monitor everything that the guest does on their device and steal data. This is why it is a good idea to avoid entering sensitive data while you are connected to a public Wi-Fi connection.

Other types of wireless attacks can be conducted via Bluetooth. One of which is bluesnarfing which is an attack that copies the target's information through Bluetooth. There is also bluejacking in which the hacker sends unsolicited messages to a victim's machine over Bluetooth. One way to protect yourself against Bluetooth based attacks is to turn Bluetooth off on your phone if you are not using it to minimize the likelihood of being targeted.

Software updates are critical for maintaining your security because these updates typically include patches which fix security flaws within the software. These patches are often fixes to publicly known security flaws, which means that if you are using an outdated version of a particular piece of software, it would be very easy for a cybercriminal to find ways to hack into the software.

While we are on the topic of software updates, you should also be mindful about using legacy systems. Legacy system refers to an outdated software or hardware that is still in use. Legacy systems can become a very serious security risk because outdated systems may not be able to be outdated to secure themselves against new cyberattacks. For example, a software which is no longer in use and is no longer receiving updates could become vulnerable to cyberattacks.

The main point to keep in mind is that hackers are individuals who look for security vulnerabilities to exploit. This is not always necessarily vulnerabilities within a system or a software. Very often hackers engage in social engineering, which exploits vulnerabilities in people as well.

4 AMERICA'S CYBERSECURITY PROBLEM

As was the case with his predecessors, President Joe Biden has had to confront the challenge of cybersecurity. Following the Colonial Pipeline incident, President Biden signed an executive order to strengthen the nation's cybersecurity defenses. It was reported in 2021 that the United States experienced an increase in ransomware attacks. These are attacks in which the hacker seizes control of digital information and holds it hostage until a ransom is paid.

Finding and stopping hackers is difficult not only because of the difficulty involved in trying to attribute cyberattacks. There is also the fact that federal laws do not specifically address ransomware attacks. Ransomware attacks are covered under the "Electronic Communications Privacy Act of 1986", as well as the "Computer Fraud and Abuse Act of 1986." That the two federal laws which address this issue are from 1986 is concerning enough, but there is also a lack of guidance on how to legally address the issue. The focus of the government has mainly been in helping to allocate resources to state and local governments. In 2018, President Donald Trump established the Cybersecurity and Infrastructure Security Agency (CISA) to improve cybersecurity across the government, but this has not done enough to address the problem of ransomware. Some states have decided to address the problem themselves by passing laws which address ransomware. Michigan passed a law which criminalized the possession of ransomware.

In a public address, President Biden warned of an incoming cyberattack from Russia. He also noted that the private sector would ultimately be the one to decide the level of technological security in the country. The private sector is not required to follow the strict cybersecurity guidelines of the government and most of America's critical infrastructure is privately owned. This includes water systems and pipelines. This means that the burden to protect the United States from cyberattacks is largely on private companies. This is why President Biden described private investment into cybersecurity as a "patriotic obligation."

The problem is that getting businesses to work with the government has been challenging. When Colonial Pipeline was targeted by a ransomware attack in 2021, it took days for Colonial Pipeline to share crucial information with CISA. Jen Easterly, the director of CISA, supported legislation which would require companies to report cyberattacks within twenty-four hours. This is because a rapid response to cyberattacks is necessary to protect the victims of such attacks.

The private businesses have not been the only challenge which CISA has faced in its short existence. The first director of CISA, Chris Krebs, was fired by Trump when he claimed that Trump's claims of electoral fraud during the election were false. Part of Biden's Build Back Better plan has included providing more funding for CISA to train and hire more staff.

Yet another problem confronting cybersecurity in the United States is the shortage of workers. A report from Marketplace Tech noted that as Biden warned businesses about cyberattacks from Russia, the cybersecurity industry has hundreds of thousands of vacancies. The vacancies cause burnout among cybersecurity workers who are under a great deal of stress. Lesley Carhart, an incident responder with Dragos, noted that alcohol was a prevalent way that professionals coped with the stress. She mentioned the problem of suicide in the field as well.

The stress that workers have endured has caused many to leave the industry altogether. This in turn creates a situation where cybersecurity professionals are leaving the field to find other careers. This makes filling these vacancies a very difficult task. Carhart argued that senior leadership needs to take professional burnout seriously by providing mental health resources. Ultimately, it seems that what really needs to be done is that vacancies in the field need to be filled so that professionals are not overwhelmed with the workload that they are dealing with.

Cybersecurity infrastructure in the United States is a very serious issue, as was demonstrated by the Colonial Pipeline attack. President Biden's warnings about Russia demonstrate that the problem could have geopolitical consequences as well. President Biden has taken some steps to address the problem, but more certainly needs to be done. Not only are clearer laws needed, but within the field vacant positions need to be filled and working conditions need to be improved.

5 THE IDEOLOGY OF NORTH KOREA

In 2002, President George W. Bush declared that North Korea was part of the "Axis of Evil" along with Iraq and Iran. This speech was a very clear public indication of Bush's aggressive policy towards North Korea. Bush's remark came weeks before a scheduled trip to South Korea where Bush would meet with President Kim Dae-jung. Bush's objective was to get South Korea to adopt a more confrontational policy regarding North Korea. The policy pursued by President Bush placed a strain on America's relationship with South Korea. When Bush visited South Korea in 2002, Kim Dae-jung reminded Bush that the South Korean people would pay the price if the Korean War resumed. South Korea opposed America's pursuit of regime change in North Korea.

The Bush administration was also concerned with preventing North Korea from developing nuclear weapons. North Korea became concerned that the Bush administration was working to destroy its government. This in fact was the objective of the administration, as admitted by John Bolt who slapped a book titled *The End of North Korea* on a table. "That," Bolton explained, "is our policy." This policy only emboldened the regime in North Korea which expanded its nuclear arsenal during Bush's presidency. In 2003, North Korea expressed a willingness to halt its nuclear weapons program if the United States agreed to sign a non-aggression treaty, but this proposal was rejected by the United States.

North Korea would have a similarly tense relationship with Bush's successor, Barack Obama. The tension between the two nations was demonstrated by an incident involving a movie titled *The Interview*. The movie was a parody film produced by Sony which depicted the assassination of North Korea's leader, Kim Jong-un. The government of North Korea was not pleased by this film. North Korea sent a letter to the United Nations which described the film as an "act of war". There was some consternation about the film within Sony, but Sony decided to move ahead with releasing the film.

North Korea responded by launching a cyberattack against

Sony. The attack was carried out via phishing emails which were sent to employees at Sony. The attackers established phony websites to harvest credentials which allowed them to gain access to Sony's systems. The attack was carried out by a group calling themselves the Guardians of Peace. This group not only managed to hack its way into Sony's system, but they also exfiltrated Sony's protected contact. Some of this information—which included unreleased movies and scripts, as well as social security numbers and employee medical records—was leaked publicly. The attackers did more than steal data. After the data had been exfiltrated, the attackers modified Sony's computers and servers. This included corrupting the system's disk drivers by removing low-level information needed for booting up. Michael Lynton explained: "The folks who did this didn't just steal practically everything from the house; they burned the house down."

The Guardians of Peace used a combination of spear-phishing, malware deployment, and destructive cyberattacks to accomplish their task. Reports on the attack indicated that they leveraged custom malware to wipe Sony's systems, making data unrecoverable. They also demonstrated a strategic use of leaked information to embarrass executives, damage relationships, and increase public pressure on Sony.

The Guardians of Peace demanded that theaters pull the film and suggested that theaters that refused to do so should "remember the 11th of September 2001." Theaters did begin pulling the movie. President Obama publicly stated that the American government was able to confirm that the attack was carried out by North Korea. This was followed by sanctions against North Korea. Critics argued that the sanctions were ineffective and weakly implemented. North Korea also experienced the internet going down for eight hours. The American government did not admit any involvement in North Korea's internet going down, though there was speculation that this was a denial-of-service attack by the American government as a form of retaliation.

The attack on Sony certainly was not the only example of North Korea carrying out a cyberattack of such nature. In May 2017, the WannaCry attack was launched. This malicious attack infected hundreds of thousands of computers across more than 150 countries within days. The attack was later attributed to North

Korean state-sponsored hackers.

From the American perspective, North Korea is part of what Bush called the "Axis of Evil." North Korea is a nation which has been run by a brutal and oppressive dictatorship. North Korea has been described as "a failing Stalinist dictatorship held together only by the ruthless repression of a mad ruler who dreams of firing nuclear weapons at Los Angeles." American foreign policy towards North Korea is one which has generally viewed North Korea as a threat to be isolated and eliminated. It is true that the regime in North Korea has been a brutal one centered around a dynastic personality cult which has sanctioned human rights abuses, such as kidnapping Japanese citizens. Even so, the American depictions of North Korea have tended to overlook how North Korea's historical experiences and its ideology has shaped both North Korea's domestic policies and its relationship with the rest of the world.

In the first place, one must understand the history of how foreign powers have shaped the politics of Korea. Grace Lee provided a short summary: "Strategically located at a peninsular tip of the East Asian continent, Korea has long been a pawn of contention between its two powerful neighbors, China and Japan. From the earliest recorded history, the Korean people have fought fiercely to maintain their independence in the face of multiple invasions by Mongols, Manchurians, Han Chinese and Japanese pirates and samurais. The sum total of these invasions may qualify Korea as the most oft-invaded territory in the world. Under the Yi Dynasty, which ruled Korea from 1392 until the Japanese annexation in 1910, Korea became a highly defensive state with a foreign policy of isolation towards the outside world. When Kim Il Sung came to power in North Korea in 1945, he arguably reverted to the highly isolationist policies of pre-modern Korea."

North Korea was founded by Kim Il Jung. Kim Il Sung promoted an ideology known as Chuche (or Juche). This was an ideology which was rooted in Korean culture and ideas, such as Confucianism. Kim Il Sung had described the ideology as follows: "Establishing *juche* means, in a nutshell, being the master of revolution and reconstruction in one's own country. This means holding fast to an independent position, rejecting dependence on others, using one's own brains, believing in one's own strength, displaying the revolutionary spirit of self-reliance, and thus solving one's own problems for oneself on one's own responsibility under all circumstances."

Chuche is an ideology which promotes the idea that the Korean masses are the masters of their country's development. As such, Chuche promoted self-reliance. A curious contradiction of the regime in North Korea is that Kim Il Sung promoted self-reliance, even though the North Korean government was heavily dependent on aid from other socialist countries. This aid was not officially recognized, however.

A report from the Embassy of Hungary in North Korea to the Hungarian Foreign Ministry noted: "Comrade Puzanov said that the Soviet Union does not need constant expressions of gratitude for its help, but the Korean comrades are displaying too 'modest' behavior concerning the assistance, and they try to hush it up." The report noted that Kim Il Sung personally requested assistance with his Five-year plan. Such aid to North Korea was considered important not only because of what it "can mean for the development of a previously backward and colonial country," but also because of the achievements which resulted from the American aid to South Korea.

The same report from the Embassy of Hungary also noted that North Korea's attempt to conceal the aid would ultimately be unsuccessful, stating: "It could be that they wish to emphasize to South Korea the independence of the DPRK in all respects, or that they have some other ideas. Comrade Kohousek remarked that any bourgeois economist can easily calculate that the DPRK was unable to reach its achievements on its own, and it is similarly unable to provide the economic aid it recently offered to South Korea from its own resources. In his opinion, the Korean comrades will achieve just the opposite with this, and their proposals can be more easily labeled 'Communist propaganda.'"

In the 1990s, it became undeniable that North Korea's economy was dependent on foreign support. It was expected that the collapse of the Soviet Union would result in a collapse of the regime in North Korea. This was not the case, though the fall of the Soviet Union did result in North Korea suffering a devastating economic blow. The Soviet Union had subsidized organizations which traded with North Korea, but this policy changed in the 1990s when Russia demanded that North Korea pay international market prices for Russian goods and services. China adopted a similar policy toward North Korea as well.

The economic disaster impacted agriculture in North Korea. North Korea's agriculture was heavily dependent on cheap oil and spare parts from the Soviet Union to run electric pump irrigation systems. Without the Soviet aid, North Korea faced an energy crisis which reduced agricultural production. The energy crisis combined with floods led to a famine in the country. The precise number of those killed is not known, though it is estimated that the number of those killed ranges from 500,000 to 3 million.

The economic collapse has led to other issues as well, such as the rapid increase of corruption in North Korea in the 1990s. Prior to the 1990s, strict regulations made private business impossible since items such as apartments and cars could not be purchased with cash, but these restrictions were no longer enforced. This led to officials taking bribes. In some cases, low ranking officials faced starvation themselves.

The economic hardships which North Korea experienced following the fall of the Soviet Union clearly demonstrated why self-reliance was necessary. Self-reliance was something which Kim Il Sung promoted, but which he was not able to successfully achieve for North Korea.

North Korea relied heavily on aid from socialist nations and had presented itself as a socialist nation, although following the economic struggles which North Korea faced in the 1990s, the limits of socialism in North Korea had been clearly exposed as Andrei Lankov explained: "The commonly held notion of North Korea as the only remaining Communist (or Stalinist or socialist) dictatorship on the planet is largely outdated. At the moment, North Korea looks like a poorly developed market economy characterized by extensive government intervention and heavy but inconsistent regulation."

North Korea described Chuche as Kim Il Sung's application of Marxist-Leninist principles to the political realities in North Korea, but there is certainly more to Chuche than this. After all, despite the fact that North Korea is officially known as the Democratic Republic of Korea, there is little that is democratic about it. Kim Il Sung established a family dynasty, which is quite unusual for a Marxist-Leninist state, especially considering that family dynasties were an aspect of the previous feudal Choson Dynasty which ruled Korea. Nicolas Levi explained that even "after the demise of the 500-year Choson Kingdom in 1910, North Korea still adheres to a dynastic system."

Chuche not only promoted self-reliance, but political and ideological independence. This meant political and ideological independence from the Soviet Union and China. Kim Il Sung stated that North Koreans must "resolutely repudiate the tendency to swallow things of others undigested or imitate them mechanically." In time, Kim Il Sung would accuse both China and the Soviet Union of abandoning the principles of Marxism-Leninism, which demonstrated his ideological independence from both nations. Of course, such remarks were ironic coming from Kim Il Sung, whose ideology deviated greatly from Marxism-Leninism.

Kim Il Sung was apparently greatly influenced by the ideas of Mao Zedong, though this is something which Kim Il Sung never acknowledged publicly. Kim Il Sung was trained in the Chinese communist guerilla army from 1935 to 1941. Many scholars have suggested that Kim was also a member of the Chinese Communist Party. Despite the early Chinese influences on Kim Il Sung, the influence of Confucianism in North Korea demonstrated a very significant difference between the ideology of Kim Il Sung and that of Mao.

Nicolas Levi explained: "Confucianism had been both the religion and ideology of the state for centuries. Choson Dynasty Confucianism was not only a philosophical and ethical system but also a cult of the family. Everyone was expected to show filial piety towards their parents, ancestors and the king. Participation in family sacrifices helped link the individual to the monarch, who was considered the 'father' of the national community." In China, Confucianism became one of the targets of the Cultural Revolution. In North Korea, however, Confucianism remained an important part of the political and social organization.

Confucianism is based on the relationship among family members. Sons are expected to obey their fathers, daughters obey their mothers, younger siblings obey older siblings, and wives obey their husbands. In the realm of politics, Confucianism meant that villages followed the leadership of venerated elders. Citizens were also expected to revere the ruling king, who was seen as the father of the state. Kim Il Sung was venerated as the father of the country. When Kim Il Sung died, he was succeeded by his son Kim Jong Il.

Mao's opposition to Confucianism was based on the view that Confucianism is a reactionary doctrine which sought to restore slavery in China during a period in China's history when the country shifted from slavery to feudalism. Ling Hsiao explained: "Except for the revolution led by the proletariat, only the replacement of the slave system by the feudal system actually constituted a social change in China's history which saw the dictatorship of one class replaced by that of another class in its full sense. The struggle between the Confucian and Legalist lines took place during that social change."

Ling Hsiao argued that "Mencius (390-305 B.C.), a representative of the Confucian school, came out with the theory peddling 'benevolent rule' in an attempt to negate and overthrow the political power of the new emerging landlord class and restore dictatorship of the slave-owners." Ling Hsiao continued to note that the representatives of the Legalist school refused the theory of benevolent rule by pointing out that it was aimed at "deceiving and keeping the people ignorant" and that it opposed reform.

Chin Shih Huang, the emperor who unified China under a centralized authority, adopted the Legalist line. Chin Shih Huang implemented a policy of repressing Confucianist thought in China. He burned books and buried Confucian scholars alive. Ling Hsiao regarded such measures as "revolutionary measures" because these measures were aimed at smashing the attacks being made by the slave-owners' restorationist forces. Following Chin Shih Huang's death, Chao Kao seized power in an attempt to restore the previous social order. This was followed by a peasant uprising which was led by Chen Sheng and Wu Kuang. This uprising was a blow to the attempts to restore slavery. Ling Hsiao explained that the masses "were the main force in fighting against restoration." The peasant uprising created the space for the emerging landlord class to come into being. Ling Hsiao explained that the clash between the declining slave-owning class and the landlord class continued after the formation of the Western Han Dynasty.

Ling Hsiao noted that with gradual disappearance of the danger of the restoration of slavery after the Western Han Dynasty, the landlord class began to detest the Legalist ideas and found that a modified version of Confucian ideas suited its needs. At this point, the contradiction in Chinese society was not between slave-owners and slaves, but between landlords and peasants. At this point, Confucian doctrines became the dominant ideology of the landlord class and Legalists ceased to represent the newly emerging class. Ling Hsiao noted that it became "impossible for the Legalists to solve the daily sharpening basic contradiction in feudal society and find a way out for the feudal system." In the view of Maoists in China, Confucianism was an ideology which represented the interests "of the most reactionary and darkest forces" and that Confucianism always hindered social change and social progress.

Kim Il Sung held a different view of Confucianism. He utilized the ideals of Confucianism as part of his effort to create a personality cult. In this regard, Confucian culture became a powerful propaganda tool for Kim Il Sung, who was presented as the head of the "Korean family". In North Korea, Kim Il Sung was presented as a political figure who was superior to the great religious leaders in history. The ruling party in North Korea openly proclaimed that Kim Il Sung was "superior to Christ in love, superior to Buddha in benevolence, superior to Confucius in virtue and superior to Mohamed in justice."

This emphasis on Kim Il Sung being a great individual leader was a clear break with the principles of Lenin, as Grace Lee pointed out: "*Juche* also diverges from Lenin's focus on the educating and organizing functions of the elite revolutionary vanguard. Authoritarianism is inherent in the *juche* ideology because the guidance of an 'exceptionally brilliant and outstanding leader' is considered essential to the mobilization of the masses of the working class."

Nicolas Levi explained: "The first stage of this socialist reform used many ideological slogans calling for the abolition of established feudalistic institutions but did not directly challenge the basic ideological roots of Confucianism in Korea." Kim Il Sung did not challenge the ideological roots of Confucianism in North Korea because those roots proved to be very effective in maintaining his regime.

It is also worth noting that under the leadership of Kim Il Sung, North Korea was viewed as a model for others around the world. Eldridge Cleaver stated in a pamphlet titled "On the Ideology of the Black Panther Party" that Kim Il Sung and Mao Tse-tung had injected something new into Marxism-Leninism. The Black Panther Party looked to North Korea and China as models of socialist revolutions which were led by non-white leaders such as Mao and Kim. In 1976, President Moussa Traoré of Mali visited North Korea. During the visit, he spoke about the achievements of the struggles in Indochina and Africa. President Traoré also expressed praise for Kim Il Sung and the Chuche ideology. He referred to North Korea as "a model for the developing countries."

North Korea certainly became a model to Guyana, which was led by Forbes Burnham at the time. Burnham came to power in Guyana with the support of the United States, but Burnham's relationship with the United States cooled after Burnham came to power and began promoting the ideology of "co-operative socialism." Despite claiming socialism, Burnham's relationship with other socialist nations came with challenges. The Soviet Union recognized the People's Progressive Party—one of the major opposition parties in Guyana—as a Marxist-Leninist party. This was hardly surprising given that Burnham came to power with American support and Burnham had denounced the "Soviet threat" in Guyana. The Soviet Union was clearly more favorable towards the PPP, even rejecting Burnham's bid to have his People's National Congress party join the Communist International.

Cuba was more supportive of Burnham's government in Guyana than the Soviet Union was. Cuba provided medical personnel, scholarships, and military aid. The problem for Burnham was that Cuba was also aligned with the PPP opposition party. Burnham was also concerned about the relationship between

Cubans and the Work People's Alliance, which was another opposition party in Guyana. Five Cuban diplomats were expelled from Guyana for allegedly providing guerrilla training to members of the Working People's Alliance.

North Korea proved to be a more reliable socialist ally for Burnham. Whereas Cuba and the Soviet Union promoted orthodox Marxism-Leninism, which the PNC did not practice, North Korea praised the co-operative socialism for Burnham. North Korea saw similarities between Burnham's socialist ideology and the Chuche concept which was promoted in North Korea by Kim Il Sung, particularly because the two ideologies promoted self-reliance.

Throughout the 1970s, Guyana and North Korea developed close relations. North Korea provided aid to Guyana to assist with Guyana's goal of reaching self-sufficiency. North Korea also influenced the policies of the PNC government in more direct ways. In 1979, the PNC announced Mass Games in Guyana, which were to be held on February 23, 1980. Mass Games refers to a display of arts and gymnastics.

In September 1979, a team of seven members were sent to Guyana to help prepare Guyana for Mass games. These seven individuals were headed by Kim Il Nam, who was personally selected for the mission by Kim Il Sung. The team spent several months familiarizing themselves with the history and culture of Guyana. Mass games were held by the government of Guyana throughout the 1980s under the direction of the Ministry of Education's Mass Games Secretariat.

Mass Games in Guyana was denounced by the opposition, who argued that it would "serve no educational purpose but merely to divert attention from the general economic and social situation of the country." The Working People's Alliance called on parents and teachers to boycott the event. Despite these objections, Guyana held Mass Games throughout the 1980s. By 1982, Mass Games training was incorporated into the public school system's physical education curriculum and by the mid-1980s the Guyana Defence Force was incorporated into Mass Games.

Much like in North Korea, Mass Games in Guyana was used to highlight the government and the nation's president. Mass Games in Guyana reflected the culture of Guyana, however. Yolanda Marshall, a writer and poet who performed in the 1986 Mass

Games as a dancer, explained: "Our Mass Games resembled some type of an African celebration from slavery with a mixture of militancy and blending of cultures. I personally feel my Guyanese Mass Games was more fun, after all, most Guyanese love to dance to good music." Moe Taylor gave the following description of the type of influence that Kim Il Sung had on Guyana as follows: "In the 1970s when North Korea was presenting itself as a model for Third World development, Kim Il Sung's message for countries like Guyana was that cultural development and educational reform were of even greater importance for them, as they faced the double burden of building the objective conditions of socialism and freeing themselves from the psycho-cultural legacy of colonialism."

The appeal of North Korea under the leadership of Kim Il Sung was that North Korea was a socialist nation which freed itself from Japanese imperialism and withstood the onslaught from American imperialism during the Korean War. The end of the Cold War was a period of transformation for North Korea. The regime in North Korea was forced to change in order to survive in power. As noted previously, North Korea adopted a market economy in an attempt to bolster its struggling economy. In 2001, North Korea began pursuing economic ventures with South Korea, which seemed to contradict the principle of Chuche.

The economic situation in North Korea forced certain economic reforms, but one aspect of Chuche which remained consistent under the leadership of Kim Jong Il and Kim Jong-un has been North Korea's its desire to protect itself from outside threats. Cha and Kang explained that emotion and ideology "have often interfered with the reasoned study of North Korea, and this has led scholars and policymakers to consistently overestimate the North Korean threat and to misunderstand the motivations behind North Korea's actions." That motivation has been survival in the face of a superior adversary.

References:

Andrei Lankov, "The Resurgence of a Market Economy in North

Korea," January 2016.

Antonio DeSimone and Nicholas Horton, "Sony's Nightmare Before Christmas: The 2014 North Korean Cyber Attack on Sony and Lessons for US Government Actions in Cyberspace," The Johns Hopkins University Applied Physics Laboratory LLC., 2017.

December 08, 1960 Report, Embassy of Hungary in North Korea to the Hungarian Foreign Ministry

Grace Lee, "The Political Philosophy of Juche," *Stanford Journal of East Asian Affairs*, Volume 3, no. 1, 2003.

James I. Matray, "The Failure of the Bush Administration's North Korea Policy: A Critical Analysis," *140 International Journal of Korean Studies*, 2013.

June 02, 1976 Hungarian Embassy in the DPRK, Telegram, 2 June 1976. Subject: Visit of the president of Mali in the DPRK.

Liang Hsiao, "Study the Historical Experience of the Struggle Between the Confucian and Legalist Schools," *Peking Review*, January 10, 1975.

Moe Taylor, "'Only a disciplined people can build a nation': North Korean Mass Games and Third Worldism in Guyana, 1980-1992," *The Asia-Pacific Journal*, Volume 13, Issue 4, no. 2, Jan. 26, 2015.

Nicolas Levi, "The Importance of Confucian Values to Kim Jong Il's System: A comparison with Kim Il Sung's System," 2012.

6 COLONIAL PIPELINE AND THE PATCHWORK APPROACH

In 2021 Colonial Pipeline was the victim of a ransomware attack which shutdown the pipeline for several days. On May 7, 2021, Colonial Pipeline's IT network was infiltrated by a ransomware attack which was carried out by a criminal cybercrime group operating on a ransomware-as-a-service model. The breach was traced back to a compromised virtual private network (VPN) account that lacked multi-factor authentication. This allowed the attackers to gain unauthorized access to the company's systems.

Once inside of the system, the attackers then deployed malware that encrypted critical files and demanded payment to restore access. The attack initially affected Colonial's business IT systems, but the company was uncertain about the full extent of the threat and decided to shut down pipeline operations entirely as a precaution. This shutdown was unprecedented in Colonial Pipeline's history and halted the flow of fuel to millions of consumers.

The impact of the attack was widely felt. It resulted in fuel shortages and an increase in gas prices. The situation even prompted a response from the federal government who assisted with the efforts to assist Colonial Pipeline's response to the incident. This included helping to transport gasoline to address the fuel shortage. The attack encrypted files on a computer used by Colonial Pipeline. The attackers carried out this attack by compromising a password which had been reused on a different website. This demonstrates why it is not advisable to reuse the same password across multiple platforms because if the password gets compromised on one platform, there is a chance it could be compromised on another. This is precisely what happened with Colonial Pipeline. The entire attack could have been avoided had better security measures been implemented, but this was not the case.

The hack impacted Colonial Pipeline's billing system. To protect its finances, Colonial Pipeline decided not to distribute any fuel without proper billing in place and opted to shut down operations completely. It is worth noting that the hackers specifically went after the billing system which was less secure than the systems which control and manage the line. Colonial Pipeline paid $4.4 million in ransom to the attackers before getting their system back online.

In addition to Colonial Pipeline, there have been examples of other energy industries being impacted by cybersecurity attacks. For example, in 2013 Iranian hackers were able to successfully hack into the control system of Bowman Avenue Dam near the village of Rye Brook in New York. In July 2024, the FBI released a warning to renewable industry companies and residents that a vulnerability in their solar panels left the panels vulnerable to being hacked. The panels' inverters are able to connect to home internet, which then makes them accessible to hackers who are able to change them or turn them off.

The rate at which cyberattacks on energy are taking place is alarming. In 2024, 67% of critical infrastructure which operates in energy, oil, and utility sectors were targeted by ransomware attacks. The number was identical to the attack rate which was reported in 2023. Of those who were targeted in 2024, 98% of energy companies claimed that the attackers attempted to compromise their backups during the attack and that 79% of these attempts were successful. Without the ability to access backups, energy companies are essentially forced to pay the ransom to get their data back. The mean cost of recovery from these ransomware attacks was $3.12 million.

It was evident in the aftermath of the cyberattack on Colonial Pipeline that existing regulations had failed. Prior to the attack, the cybersecurity standard for pipelines was a largely voluntary one in which it was up to pipelines to follow "best practices" out of their own best interest. There was no mandatory cybersecurity regulation for the pipeline sector. Even after the attack on Colonial Pipeline, some in the private sector have argued that cybersecurity for pipelines should remain voluntary because mandatory regulations would increase business expenses. There was also concern that any mandatory measures would become outdated and ineffective. As will be addressed later, voluntary regulations pose certain challenges which often render them ineffective, but there are legitimate concerns over mandatory regulations which are imposed through legislation and enforced through government agencies.

The federal government has struggled with implementing streamlined cybersecurity policies in part due to the decentralized nature of federal regulations. This approach has been described as a "patchwork" framework due to the lack of centralized authority. The responsibility for regulating and enforcing cybersecurity laws falls under the purview of a number of federal agencies including the Transportation Security Administration (TSA), the Federal Energy Regulatory Commission (FERC), the Securities and Exchange Commission (SEC), and the Federal Trade Commission (FTC).

Not only is there a problem regarding the fact that so many different agencies are tasked with enforcing cybersecurity regulations, but there is also the fact that none of these agencies were formed with the specific purpose of enforcing cybersecurity laws. Moreover, the United States has yet to pass a general statute requiring cybersecurity protocols to be upheld across all industries. This means that agencies are also forced to enforce cybersecurity regulations through statutes which are not specifically designed to address cybersecurity issues. This will be explored further regarding how certain courts have ruled on the FTC's and the SEC's efforts to enforce cybersecurity regulations.

The SEC was created for the purpose of providing financial regulation to protect investors and to oversee the stock market. The SEC was given the authority to regulate data security through the Gramm-Leach-Bliley Act of 1999. The SEC then expanded its cybersecurity regulation and enforcement in 2017 through the creation of a cyber unity which focuses on targeting cyber-related misconduct. In 2018, SEC released guidance for public companies establishing a duty to disclose material cybersecurity risks to investors. Since 2018, the SEC has brought enforcement actions against companies which fail to comply with these standards.

In 2018, President Donald Trump established the Cybersecurity and Infrastructure Security Agency (CISA) to improve cybersecurity across the government. CISA provided some semblance of a centralized approach to cybersecurity regulations since it is an agency which was created solely to address cybersecurity concerns. The challenge for CISA is that CISA lacks regulatory and enforcement power. CISA cannot mandate non-federal government entities to share cyber threat information. CISA also does not have subpoena power outside of the federal government.

CISA's lack of authority outside of the federal government has hindered the agency's ability to address the nation's cybersecurity concerns. This is demonstrated by a cyberattack against SolarWinds in 2020. The cyberattack injected malicious code into SolarWinds' computers. It was estimated that it took eighteen months and $100 billion for SolarWinds to fully recover. In 2021, the SEC began investigating SolarWinds under CISA's directions because CISA itself lacked the authority to conduct a direct investigation. In 2023, the SEC announced charges against SolarWinds, alleging that the company knew of the cybersecurity vulnerabilities and misled investors about the extent of these risks. Streich argued that if CISA had more centralized authority to regulate companies' cyber infrastructure, CISA may have discovered the SolarWinds hack earlier. Streich further argued that more centralized authority would also allow an agency like CISA to implement regulations such as multi-factor authentication. Multi-factor authentication could have prevented the attack on Colonial Pipeline by providing an extra layer of security.

CISA also worked alongside TSA to implement new cybersecurity guidelines for pipelines. One of the directives which the TSA issued after the Colonial Pipeline attack was that pipeline owners and operators would have to report cybersecurity incidents to CISA. Even though CISA is the agency which is better equipped to handle cybersecurity incidents, CISA itself does not have the authority to compel action from private entities, so it falls on the TSA to impose such regulations.

Following the Colonial Pipeline attack, the TSA issued a new rule which required pipelines to alert the government whenever they suffer a cyberattack. The regulation also mandated that pipeline operators must assess their own cybersecurity systems for potential weaknesses. This was the first federal cybersecurity regulation for pipeline companies, which previously only had to comply with voluntary TSA guidance which included the suggestion that such breaches be reported. This regulation came at a time when it was reported that some Democratic and Republican lawmakers were suggesting stripping oversight of pipeline security away from the TSA considering that the main duty of the TSA is to prevent terrorist attacks on airlines. The concern over having the TSA regulate the cybersecurity of pipelines was not a new concern. In 2019, two years before the Colonial Pipeline attack, the Government Accountability Office (GAO) issued a report which identified weaknesses in the TSA pipeline security guidelines. One of the issues the GAO raised was that the TSA had no process for reviewing and revising its guidelines, which meant that the TSA could not ensure that its guidelines reflect the latest standards for cybersecurity.

The TSA's role in regulating pipeline cybersecurity also led to tensions between the TSA and FERC. Two FERC commissioners expressed concern over the TSA's adequacy as a pipeline cybersecurity regulator and called for a different agency to be in charge of regulating pipeline cybersecurity. The commissioners stated that regulation should be placed in the charge of an agency which "fully comprehends the energy sector and has sufficient resources to address this growing threat." This view was supported by some members of Congress who proposed that the FERC be placed in charge of regulating pipeline cybersecurity.

The TSA measure which was passed following the 2021 attack on Colonial Pipeline was designed to penalize pipelines for failing to timely report cyberattacks, but the rule was not a preventive measure which implemented a standard to prevent cyberattacks in the first place. The attack on Colonial Pipeline was an attack which could have been prevented had different measures been taken. This reinforces the need for cybersecurity regulations which uphold a basic standard for cybersecurity protections to ensure that preventive measures are in place.

The problem with the patchwork approach is demonstrated by disagreements between the Third and Eleventh Circuits regarding the scope of the FTC's authority to enforce cybersecurity regulations. In *FTC v. Wyndham Worldwide Corp.*, the defendant suffered three cyberattacks in which hackers managed to access

Wyndham Worldwide Corporation's computer systems. The hackers stole personal and financial information for hundreds of thousands of consumers which resulted in more than $10.6 million dollars in fraudulent charges. The FTC filed a suit alleging that Wyndham's conduct was an unfair practice and that the company's privacy policy was deceptive. The FTC alleged that Wyndham had allowed hotels to store payment card information in clear readable text, that Wyndham had allowed the use of easily guessable passwords to access property management systems, and that Wyndam had failed to use "readily available security measures" such as firewalls.

The court ruled in favor of the FTC. The Third Circuit found that it should have been "painfully clear" to Wyndham that a court could find that its conduct failed the cost-benefit analysis at least after the second attack. The Third Circuit also noted that Wyndham's fair notice challenge failed because the FTC had issued a guidebook with a checklist of practices to be used. The ruling noted that Wyndham itself did not argue that the cyberattacks it suffered were unforeseeable. It would have been implausible to make such an argument given that Wyndham suffered a second and third attack after the first one. In *Wyndham*, the Third Circuit concluded that Wyndham did have fair notice that its cybersecurity practices fell short of the provision expressed in 15 U.S.C. § 45(a).

In 2018, the Eleventh Circuit upheld a motion to dismiss an FTC enforcement order against the defendant in *LabMD, Inc. v. Federal Trade Commission*. This case involved a suit against LabMD. Sometime in 2005, a peer-to-peer file sharing application called LimeWire was installed on a computer and used by LabMD's billing manager. This was contrary to LabMD's policy. In doing so, the manager had exposed the contents of her computer to other users. The personal information of 9,300 consumers were exposed.

After the breach, an investigation was launched. Subsequently a complaint was filed which alleged that LabMD committed an unfair act or practice as prohibited by Section 5(a) of the FTC Act. Rather than alleging specific acts which LabMD engaged in, the FTC complaint listed a number of data-security measures which LabMD failed to perform. Among the defenses raised by LabMD included the claim that the FTC lacked authority under Section 5 to regulate its handling of the personal information in its computer networks.

LabMD also asserted that the FTC's order was void for vagueness and that the FTC failed to provide fair notice of what data-security practices were adequate under Section 5(a). The court found the FTC's orders to implement reasonable security measures unenforceable because the FTC's enforcement action commanded LabMD to overhaul and replace its data-security program to meet "an indeterminable standard of reasonableness." The court further noted that even if LabMD's failure to implement a reasonable data-security program constituted an unfair act, the FTC failed to enjoin a specific act and its mandate for LabMD to overhaul its data-security measures did not state how this was to be done.

The cases demonstrate that there does not appear to be a clear standard for which FTC regulations are enforceable. The confusion stems from the fact that 15 U.S.C. § 45(a) is not a cybersecurity regulation. The statute is meant to regulate unfair methods of competition. This means that for a company to be found liable for violating this statute, the FTC must demonstrate that failure to engage in certain cybersecurity practices constituted an unfair practice. As the rulings in the two previously mentioned cases demonstrate, courts are split on the scope of the FTC's authority in this regard.

The disparate rulings in the two cases are concerning given that Streich noted that even though the FTC focuses on consumer protection, the FTC "is the closest thing the United States has to a central cybersecurity regulatory agency." The concern is that the FTC is the closest thing to a central cybersecurity regulatory agency, yet courts are split as to the scope of FTC's ability to regulate cybersecurity concerns. The issue is also compounded by the fact that Section 5 itself is not a cybersecurity regulation which establishes a clear standard. Instead, Section 5 allows the FTC to regulate cybersecurity standards as a part of its regulations of unfair business practices and it is up to the discretion of the courts as to whether a particular breach of cybersecurity falls within the scope of Section 5.

The other aspect of the problem is that some of the existing legislation is also outdated. For example, the Computer Fraud and Abuse Act (CFAA) was passed in 1986. The CFAA criminalizes various types of hacking, including hacking to commit espionage; hacking to commit fraud; and hacking to commit damage. CFAA has faced calls to be updated by those who argue that the law is dated and that the punishments it prescribes are often disproportionate to the crime. The situation of Aaron Swartz who faced 35 years in prison for downloading files from JSTOR is an example of CFAA's disproportionate punishment.

In 1996, Congress passed the Economic Espionage Act (EEA). EEA is narrowly focused on protecting the confidentiality of certain types of information, such as trade secrets. EEA does not apply to information which does not qualify for trade secret protection. The EEA also does not impose criminal or civil penalties on hackers who threaten the availability of information. This means that the EEA does not cover ransomware attacks.

The Electronic Communications Privacy Act (ECPA) was passed in 1986 for the purpose of governing the privacy of computer network communications. Much like the CFAA and EEA, ECPA has faced criticism for being outdated. This is hardly surprising considering that the act was passed in 1986, and electronic communication has developed very rapidly since that time. ECPA was passed at a time when Congress was concerned about new computer telecommunications which were outside the scope of the then existing laws. When ECPA was passed in 1986, the act included three parts. The first part expanded protections against wiretapping to include computer data transmissions in addition to phone calls. The second part added protection against pen registers which are used to monitor the numbers dialed from a person's phone. The third part of ECPA was a section known as the Stored Communications Act (SCA). The purpose of SCA was to create a statutory privacy right for subscribers of certain kinds of internet services.

Even though the existing law which enforces cybersecurity is lacking in many areas, such laws are necessary. Leaving private industries to regulate themselves has proven to be ineffective. This was demonstrated by the previously mentioned attack on Colonial Pipeline which could have been prevented had a simple cybersecurity measure been implemented. There are other issues with private regulations, however. One such issue is the challenges associated with litigation.

The logic of allowing private companies to regulate themselves is that it would be in the best interest of such companies to do so because failure to do so could have adverse consequences, but this is not always the case. Lawsuits are one means to compel action on the part of private companies. The threat of costly litigation is often enough to ensure that private businesses act in accordance with the law, but within the area of cybersecurity this is not always so easy. As was noted previously, the FTC's scope when it comes to regulating cybersecurity violations is limited by the fact that the FTC does not rely on statutes which are primarily focused on cybersecurity problems. The same is also true of the SEC. This means that federal agencies cannot solely be replied on to compel action through litigation.

The limitation of using litigation as a means of regulating private companies is demonstrated by Colonial Pipeline's situation. Following the previously mentioned cyberattack, Colonial Pipeline faced several lawsuits. Among the lawsuits was one filed by Ramon Dickerson who brought a negligence class action suit against Colonial Pipeline. This lawsuit alleged that Colonial Pipeline had a duty of care to use reasonable means to secure its computer systems. Another class action lawsuit was filed by a gas station known as EZ Mart 1, LLC. This lawsuit was brought by all gas stations which experienced a fuel shortage, an increase in the price of gas, or an inability to sell fuel due to the cyberattack. This class action lawsuit was also a negligence claim like the lawsuit brought by Dickerson.

The plaintiffs in the *EZ Mart 1* case struggled to establish a duty and standard of care which was rooted in common law torts. The court found that Colonial Pipeline owed no duty to EZ Mart. The court found that since EZ Mart had no relationship with Colonial Pipeline, the damages which EZ Mart alleged were not causally connected to the breach of a duty to safeguard information.

The plaintiffs in both *Dickerson* and *EZ Mart 1* had their claims rejected under the Pure Economic Loss doctrine. In both cases, the litigants alleged that their damages were related to the rising price of gas which was caused by the shortage. This principle was recognized under Georgia law. This allowed for plaintiffs to recover economic losses which result from an injury to his person or property. The problem for the plaintiffs in both cases was that cybersecurity harms do not typically result in injury to person or property. For this reason, the litigants were unable to demonstrate a cognizable harm which arose out of the cyberattack. The rulings of both cases effectively held that Colonial Pipeline was not negligent for the damages which resulted from the cyberattack. That the attack could have been mitigated or even prevented had Colonial Pipeline implemented better cybersecurity measures was not enough for Colonial Pipeline to have been found to have breached a duty to the plaintiffs who brought the cases.

There is also a barrier regarding the ability for plaintiffs to bring claims for cybercrimes. Some courts only allow lawsuits if the plaintiffs have suffered actual harm rather than a potential future harm. The Third Circuit in *Reilly v. Ceridian Corp.* held that the plaintiff did not have standing to sue Ceridian over a security breach which Ceridian suffered. Ceridian released a statement informing potential identity theft victims that some of their information may have been accessed illegally, but the court held that the plaintiffs lacked standing because their contentions relied on the possibility that their personal information had been read. The court held that unless the conjectures had come true, then the plaintiffs had no standing. Other courts have allowed suits for potential future harms. In *Krottner v. Starbucks*, the Ninth Circuit held that plaintiffs whose information had been stolen, but not misused, have suffered an injury which was sufficient enough to give them standing under Article III. These differing approaches further demonstrate the lack of a clear standard for how cybersecurity regulations are to be upheld within the judicial system. This also further contributes to the problems with the patchwork approach to cybersecurity in the United States.

7 THE LIMITS OF AMERICAN DATA PRIVACY LAWS

One of the most significant problems with data privacy law in the United States is the lack of a single, comprehensive, federal statute governing personal data. Unlike the European Union's General Data Protection Regulation (GDPR) which establishes a uniform rules across member states, the United States relies on a patchwork of sector-specific laws. For example, the Health Insurance Portability and Accountability Act (HIPAA) governs health data, the Gramm-Leach-Bliley Act (GLBA) covers certain financial information, and the Children's Online Privacy Protection Act (COPPA) addresses data related to minors.

This patchwork approach has resulted in a fragmented system which leaves gaps in protection. Take for example the previously mentioned COPPA. One major weakness of COPPA is that it was crafted before the expansion of social media. The law focuses on traditional identifiers such as names, email addresses, and phone numbers, whereas modern data collection relies heavily on behavioral tracking, algorithms, and inferred data. COPPA was passed in 1998 in response to growing concerns over the dissemination of children's personal information over the internet. The act, which applied to children under the age of thirteen, mandated that websites are required to obtain "verifiable parental consent" before collecting or using the personal information of children. COPPA is enforced by the FTC.

One of the limitations of COPPA is that it does not provide clear guidance for what is defined as a website which is directed towards children, which means that web operators must judge for themselves it they should comply with COPPA. Some websites decided to avoid the problem by removing services which could draw the attention of children. Yet another problem associated with COPPA's restrictions is that children could simply lie about their age to access adult sites.

Parental consent is the core enforcement mechanism of COPPA, but it is also one of its weakest elements. In practice, consent is obtained through methods that do not ensure genuine parental understanding or involvement. Parents may click through consent forms without fully comprehending how their child's data will be collected, shared, or retained. This turns consent into a procedural requirement rather than a meaningful safeguard.

The problems surrounding data privacy laws in the United States stem largely from an outdated and fragmented legal framework that has failed to adapt to the realities of a data-driven society. Inconsistent protections, weak consent standards, limited enforcement, and technological change all contribute to a system that places personal privacy at risk. As digital technologies continue to shape daily life, the need for more comprehensive federal data privacy law are very clear.

www.ingramcontent.com/pod-product-compliance
Lightning Source LLC
LaVergne TN
LVHW051625050326
832903LV00033B/4664